BHUTAN 2016 HUMAN RIGHTS REPORT

EXECUTIVE SUMMARY

Bhutan is a democratic, constitutional monarchy. King Khesar Namgyel Wangchuck is the head of state, with executive power vested in the cabinet, headed by Prime Minister Tshering Tobgay. In July 2013 the country held its second general elections, in which the former opposition People's Democratic Party gained a majority of the seats in the National Assembly, resulting in the country's first democratic transfer of power to the opposition. International election observers reported the elections were generally free and fair.

Civilian authorities maintained effective control over the security forces.

Principal human rights problems included discriminatory treatment of religious and ethnic minorities and the government's refusal to readmit certain refugees that asserted claims to Bhutanese citizenship.

Other human rights problems included continued incarceration of Nepali-speaking political prisoners arrested for alleged participation in antigovernment protests in the early 1990s, domestic violence, restrictions on freedom of assembly and association, social stigma against persons with disabilities, laws prohibiting consensual same-sex sexual activity, and reports of abuse of domestic workers.

There were no reports of impunity by government security forces. There have been cases of police personnel charged under civil and criminal procedures. There have been no reports of criminal charges against military personnel.

Section 1. Respect for the Integrity of the Person, Including Freedom from:

a. Arbitrary Deprivation of Life and other Unlawful or Politically Motivated Killings

There were no reports that the government or its agents committed arbitrary or unlawful killings.

b. Disappearance

There were no reports of politically motivated disappearances.

c. Torture and Other Cruel, Inhuman, or Degrading Treatment or Punishment

The constitution prohibits such practices, and there were no reports that government officials employed them.

Prison and Detention Center Conditions

Prison and detention center conditions generally met international standards.

Physical Conditions: According to police, there were no separate prisons designated for women and children.

Administration: Police administer the prison system; there was no available information regarding recordkeeping on prisoners.

Independent Monitoring: No international human rights groups sought access to monitor prisons during the year. The International Committee for the Red Cross (ICRC) has not renewed its memorandum of understanding with the Government of Bhutan since 2012 and did not request access to prisons during the reporting period.

d. Arbitrary Arrest or Detention

The law prohibits arbitrary arrest or detention, and the government generally observed these prohibitions.

Role of the Police and Security Apparatus

The Royal Bhutan Police (RBP) is responsible for internal security. The Royal Bhutan Army (RBA) is responsible for defending against external threats but also has responsibility for some internal security functions, including counterinsurgency operations, protection of forests, and security for prominent persons. The RBP reports to the Ministry of Home and Cultural Affairs, and the king is the supreme commander in chief of the RBA.

Civilian authorities maintained effective control over the army and police, and the government has effective mechanisms to investigate and punish abuse and corruption. There were no reports of impunity involving security forces during the year. The army and police have procedures to conduct internal investigations of alleged personnel misconduct. Official courts of inquiry adjudicate the allegations. The king or a senior official makes the final determination on the outcome of a case.

By law the Police Service Board, made up of senior police personnel and a Ministry of Home and Cultural Affairs representative, investigates cases of abuse. Police officers can face criminal prosecution for human rights violations. The RBP has institutional reviews, human rights training, and accountability procedures for its personnel. The Civil and Criminal Procedure Code (CCPC) also provides an avenue to check on any abuse of power in criminal investigations by an investigating officer of the RBP.

Arrest Procedures and Treatment of Detainees

Under the law, police may only arrest a person with a court-issued warrant or probable cause. Police generally respected the law. Police may perform "stop and frisk" searches only with a reasonable suspicion that a crime has been committed. Arresting authorities must issue an immediate statement of charges and engage in reasonable efforts to inform the family of the accused. The law requires authorities to bring an arrested person before a court within 24 hours, exclusive of travel time from the place of arrest. The law provides for prompt access to a lawyer and government provision of an attorney for indigent clients. Bail is available depending on the severity of charges and the suspect's criminal record, flight risk, and potential threat to the public. In addition, bail can be granted after the execution of the bail bond agreement. Remanded suspects can be held in police custody for 10 days pending investigation, which the court can extend to 49 days, and then again to 108 days in cases involving "heinous" crimes, should the investigating officer show adequate grounds. The law expressly prohibits pretrial detention beyond 108 days. Detainees may pursue a writ of habeas corpus to obtain a court-ordered release. Under the Anticorruption Act of Bhutan, an Anticorruption Commission is empowered to arrest without a warrant any person upon reasonable suspicion of the person having committed or about to commit an offense. The arrested individual must make a court appearance within 24 hours.

e. Denial of Fair Public Trial

The law provides for an independent judiciary, and the government generally respected judicial independence.

Trial Procedures

The law stipulates that defendants must receive fair, speedy, and public trials, and the government generally respected this right. A preliminary hearing must be convened within 10 days of registration of a criminal matter with the appropriate court. Before registering any plea, courts must determine whether the accused is mentally sound and understands the consequences of entering a plea. Defendants enjoy a presumption of innocence, have the right to confront witnesses, and cannot be compelled to testify; cases must be proved beyond a reasonable doubt to obtain convictions. The government has prescribed a standing rule for all courts to clear all cases within a year of the case filing. The country has an inquisitorial judicial system, and there is no trial by jury.

Defendants have the right to appeal to the High Court and may make a final appeal to the king, who traditionally delegates the decision to the Royal Advisory Council. Trials are conducted publicly although a court can order that press and the public be removed from the courtroom for part or all of the trial in the interest of justice. The law grants defendants and their attorneys access to state evidence. The court must provide the opportunity for the parties to present relevant evidence, including witness testimony. Prosecutors and defendants are allowed to conduct direct and cross-examination.

Cases are tried pursuant to the CCPC. State-appointed prosecutors for the attorney general generally are responsible for filing charges and prosecuting cases for offenses against the state. In some cases other government departments, such as the Anticorruption Commission (ACC), file charges and conduct prosecutions.

The law provides for the right to representation. Although this occurred frequently in criminal cases, in civil cases most defendants and plaintiffs represented themselves. The law states that criminal defendants may choose legal representation from a list of licensed advocates. The government promoted the use of judiciary websites for legal information as a means of self-help for defendants. There were no reports that the courts denied any groups the right to trial.

Political Prisoners and Detainees

Nongovernmental organizations (NGOs) claimed that 28 political prisoners remained in Chamgang Central Jail in Thimphu. Most political prisoners were Nepali-speaking persons associated with protests in the early 1990s. Bhutanese officials claim those remaining in prison were convicted of violent crimes during demonstrations. The government reported that as of December 2016, there were

57 prisoners serving sentences resulting from convictions under the National Security Act or its related penal code provisions. No international monitors sought access to these prisoners. Since 2010 the government has released 47 political prisoners, including one granted amnesty by the king.

Civil Judicial Procedures and Remedies

The CCPC governs the resolution of criminal trials and civil litigation and states that a suit may be initiated by a litigant or a member of the litigant's family. The CCPC also provides for compensation to those detained or subjected to unlawful detention but later acquitted. Often local or community leaders assisted in resolving minor disputes. As plaintiffs and defendants often represented themselves in civil matters, judges typically took an active role in investigating and mediating civil disputes. The CCPC does not include a provision for appeal to regional human rights bodies.

f. Arbitrary or Unlawful Interference with Privacy, Family, Home, or Correspondence

The constitution states that a person "shall not be subjected to arbitrary or unlawful interference with his or her privacy, family, home, or correspondence, or to unlawful attacks on the person's honor and reputation." The government generally respected these prohibitions.

Section 2. Respect for Civil Liberties, Including:

a. Freedom of Speech and Press

The law provides for freedom of speech and press. Citizens could publicly and privately criticize the government without reprisal.

Freedom of Speech and Expression: The constitution provides for freedom of speech including for members of the press. Defamation can carry criminal penalties, and citizens were cautious in their expression, especially as it related to criticism of the royal family or government practices.

Press and Media Freedoms: The media law does not provide specific protections for journalists or guarantee freedom of information. The media law also prohibits media outlets from supporting political parties. Media sources suggested that while there was commitment to media freedom at the highest levels, some media professionals continued to find bureaucrats unwilling to share information, especially on issues of corruption and violations of the law. Independent media outlets relied heavily on government advertisements for revenue, and most news outlets struggled to generate sufficient revenue to operate.

Censorship or Content Restrictions: In its *Freedom in the World 2016* report, Freedom House reported that a 2015 survey of 119 current and former Bhutanese journalists revealed general concerns about press freedom and access to information. Local contacts reported increased use of social media to raise complaints of official misconduct or abuse.

Internet Freedom

The government generally permitted individuals and groups to engage in peaceful expression of views via the internet. Government officials stated the government did not block access, restrict content, or censor websites. Freedom House reported the government occasionally blocked access to websites containing pornography or information deemed offensive to the state. Such blocked information typically did not extend to political content. The Annual Statistics 2015 of the Ministry of Information and Communications estimated the number of internet users at 61.15 percent of the population.

Academic Freedom and Cultural Events

There were no government restrictions on academic freedom and cultural events.

b. Freedom of Peaceful Assembly and Association

Freedom of Assembly

While the constitution provides for the right to assemble peacefully, the government restricted this right. The 1992 National Security Act permits the government to control the public's right to assembly "to avoid breaches of the peace" by requiring licenses, prohibiting assembly in designated areas, and declaring curfew. The penal code prohibits "promotion of civil unrest" as an act that is prejudicial to the maintenance of harmony among different nationalities, racial groups, castes, or religious groups.

Freedom of Association

The constitution provides for freedom of association, and the government permitted the registration of some political parties and organizations that were deemed "not harmful to the peace and unity of the country." Many of the NGOs in the country maintained formal or informal connections to members of the royal family. In its Freedom in the World 2016 report, Freedom House stated the government did not permit the operation of NGOs working on the status of Nepali-speaking refugees. Under the law, all NGOs must register with the government. In order to register an NGO, an individual must be a Bhutanese citizen, disclose his or her family income and assets, disclose his or her educational qualifications, and disclose any criminal records.

c. Freedom of Religion

See the Department of State's *International Religious Freedom Report* at www.state.gov/religiousfreedomreport/.

d. Freedom of Movement, Internally Displaced Persons, Protection of Refugees, and Stateless Persons

The law provides for freedom of internal movement, foreign travel, emigration, and repatriation, but the government limited freedom of movement and repatriation. Freedom of movement often was restricted along ethnic lines. Rules established differences in citizenship categories and determined whether a person may be granted a "route permit" to travel internally or obtain a passport for international travel. (Bhutanese citizens are required to obtain a security clearance certificate to obtain a passport.)

Foreign Travel: The law establishes different categories of citizenship under which foreign travel is restricted. NGOs reported these restrictions primarily affected ethnic Nepalis although children of single mothers who could not establish citizenship through a Bhutanese father were also affected.

Exile: The law does not address forced exile, and there were no reported cases of forced exile during the year. In the early 1990s, the government reportedly forced between 80,000 and 100,000 Nepali-speaking residents to leave the country, following a series of decisions taken during the 1970s and 1980s establishing legal requirements for Bhutanese citizenship.

As of September after years of international resettlement efforts, approximately 10,000 Nepali-speaking refugees remained in two refugee camps in Nepal administered by the Office of the UN High Commissioner for Refugees (UNHCR). In its *Freedom in the World 2016* report, Freedom House stated, 18,000 Nepali-speaking refugees remain in Nepal as of late 2015. The Bhutanese government claimed UNHCR failed to screen individuals who originally entered these camps to determine whether they had any ties to Bhutan.

Emigration and Repatriation: There continued to be delays in government consideration of claims to Bhutanese citizenship by refugees in Nepal.

Citizenship: Under the constitution, only children whose parents can both be proven to be citizens of Bhutan can apply for citizenship up to their first birthday, after which a petition must be filed with the king to be granted citizenship. NGOs reported that approximately 9,000 applicants have received citizenship since 2006. In May, 163 persons from Tashichhodzong and in August, 93 from Mongar were granted citizenship by the king. The law provides for revocation of the citizenship of any naturalized citizen who "has shown by act or speech to be disloyal in any manner whatsoever to the king, country, and people." The law permits reapplication for citizenship after a two-year probationary period. The government can restore citizenship after successful completion of the probation and a finding that the individual was not responsible for any act against the government.

Protection of Refugees

Access to Asylum: The law does not provide for the granting of asylum or refugee status, and the government has not established a system for providing protection to refugees.

The Central Tibetan Administration (CTA) reported that since the 1960s the country had sheltered Tibetan refugees who were initially located in seven settlements. The government reported that the Tibetans were integrated into society and that approximately 1,600 had applied for and received citizenship. As of July, there were 2,583 Tibetan refugees as per records maintained by the Department of Immigration. There are no current records of these refugees holding work permits. The CTA did not have an official presence in the country and did not provide social and economic assistance to Tibetans in Bhutan. The country's border with China was closed, and Tibetans generally did not transit the country en route to India. The Tibetan population in the country appears stable. It is decreasing as Tibetan refugees adopt Bhutanese citizenship according to the Department of Immigration.

<u>Employment</u>: There were unconfirmed reports that some Tibetan refugees and some Nepali-speaking Bhutanese citizens could not obtain security clearances for government jobs, enroll in higher education, or obtain licenses to run private businesses. According to the government, all Bhutanese citizens are eligible for security clearances provided they do not have criminal records.

<u>Access to Basic Services</u>: The government stated that Tibetan refugees have the same access to government-provided health care and education as citizens, and access was given routinely. According to the CTA, 13 Tibetan refugees have received licenses to run businesses. The CTA also said that while Tibetan refugees are not eligible for government employment, a few Tibetan refugees worked as teachers and health-care providers under temporary government contracts. They reportedly have difficulties traveling within and outside the country.

<u>Durable Solutions</u>: Tibetan refugees could travel to India although many faced obstacles in obtaining travel permits. There were also reports the government did not provide the travel documents necessary for Tibetan refugees to travel beyond India. The government continued to delay implementing a process to identify and repatriate refugees with claims to Bhutanese residency or citizenship.

Stateless Persons

A nationwide census in 1985 resulted in a determination that many Nepali-speaking persons in Bhutan were not citizens, effectively rendering them stateless. The government alleged that they were not citizens because they could not prove they had been resident in the country in 1958. The census was repeated in 1988-89 in the southern districts. During the second round of the census, those who were deemed not to be citizens in 1985 could apply for citizenship provided they met certain conditions. Those who did not meet the new criteria were categorized by the government as illegal immigrants and expelled. According to NGOs, an unknown number of Nepali-speaking stateless persons remained in the country, mainly in the south.

NGOs and media sources also highlighted the existence of stateless children born to unwed mothers who were unable to prove the identity of the father of the child. According to 2014 NGO reports, more than 700 children born in the country were not recognized as Bhutanese citizens because the nationality of their fathers was undocumented. Nonetheless, the Bhutanese government claimed that 20 children in the kingdom fell into this category.

Stateless persons cannot obtain "no objection certificates" and security clearance certificates, which are often necessary for access to public healthcare, employment, access to primary and secondary education, enrollment at institutions of higher education, travel documents, and business ownership. According to contacts, approximately 1,000 families are stateless. The National Commission for Women and Children stated children without citizenship were eligible for public educational and health services.

Section 3. Freedom to Participate in the Political Process

The constitution provides citizens the right to choose their government peacefully, and citizens exercised this right through periodic, free, and fair elections based on universal and equal suffrage.

Elections and Political Participation

Recent Elections: The government successfully held national elections in July 2013. Voters elected the country's second National Assembly, the lower house of parliament. The opposition People's Democratic Party won 32 of 47 seats, ousting the former ruling party, the Druk Phensum Tshogpa. International observers generally considered the elections free and fair; there were no reports of significant irregularities during the election process.

Political Parties and Political Participation: The constitution states that political parties shall promote national unity and shall not resort to regionalism, ethnicity, or religion to incite voters for electoral gain. Political parties are required to be broad-based, have a national membership, not be limited to a particular regional or other demographic constituency, and not receive money or other assistance from foreign sources. To run for office, party candidates must possess a university degree and resign from a civil service job if held. Individuals who resign from the civil service cannot re-enter the service. While only two political parties contested the 2008 national elections, five parties contested the 2013 elections. The government provided funding only for general elections and maintained rigid guidelines on party financing.

Participation of Women and Minorities: As part of the country's strict separation of religion from politics, the law barred ordained members of the clergy, including Buddhist monks and nuns, from participating in politics, including voting and running for office. There were no other laws limiting the participation of women and members of minorities in the political process.

Section 4. Corruption and Lack of Transparency in Government

The law provides criminal penalties for corruption by officials, and the government generally implemented these laws effectively. There were isolated reports of government corruption during the year. The 2011 Anticorruption Act, which is based on the UN Convention against Corruption, expands the mandate of the ACC to cover the private sector and enhances the ACC's investigatory powers and functions.

Corruption: The government took an active role in addressing official corruption through the Public Accounts Committee in the National Assembly and the Royal Audit Authority, which monitored the use of government funds. The ACC is authorized to investigate cases of official corruption and allows citizens to post information on its website regarding corrupt practices. The ACC reportedly faced resource constraints. The constitution enables the ACC to act as an independent body although its investigative staff was primarily civil servants answerable to the Royal Civil Service Commission. In July 2015, the prime minister removed the foreign minister from his post due to a corruption scandal related to a charge of embezzlement of public property during Foreign Minister's Rinzin Dorje past tenure as governor of Haa Province. Freedom House stated that Dorje was convicted and sentenced to one year in prison on September 2015. He was acquitted on July 28 of all charges by the Supreme Court.

Financial Disclosure: The law requires public servants, and persons working for NGOs using public resources, their spouses, and dependents to declare their income, assets, and liabilities.

Public Access to Information: The constitution mandates a right to information; however, no law provides for public access to government information. Several ministries publish laws, regulations, budgets, and other relevant information on websites to enhance transparency.

Section 5. Governmental Attitude Regarding International and Nongovernmental Investigation of Alleged Violations of Human Rights

According to international NGOs, local civil society organizations practiced self-censorship to avoid issues perceived as sensitive by the government. Sensitive issues included women's rights and environmental issues. The government reportedly did not permit human rights groups established by the Nepali-speaking community to operate, categorizing them as political organizations that did not promote national unity.

The United Nations or Other International Bodies: An agreement between the government and the International Committee of the Red Cross (ICRC) allowing the ICRC to make prison visits to persons detained for crimes against the security of the state expired in 2013 and was not renewed. The ICRC continued to engage with the government to facilitate prison visits for Bhutanese refugees living in Nepal. The UN has a resident coordinator in Bhutan, and UN organizations, including the UN Development Program and UN Children's Fund, have a strong presence.

Government Human Rights Bodies: The National Assembly Human Rights Committee (NAHRC) conducted human rights research on behalf of the National Assembly. The Civil Society Organization (CSO) Authority has the legal authority to regulate civil society operations. Forty-seven CSOs were registered, of which 35 were categorized as Public Benefit Organizations and 12 Mutual Benefit Organizations.

Section 6. Discrimination, Societal Abuses, and Trafficking in Persons

Women

Rape and Domestic Violence: The law defines criminal sexual assault and specifies penalties. In cases of rape involving minors, sentences range from five to 15 years in prison. In extreme cases a person convicted of rape may be imprisoned for life. According to NGOs, cultural taboos and a lack of rights awareness among survivors resulted in underreporting of rapes. Spousal rape is illegal and prosecuted as a misdemeanor. The government criminalized the traditional practice of "night hunting" (bomena), practiced mainly in the eastern parts of country, in which a man climbs into a single woman's window to have sex with her. According to the National Commission for Women and Children (NCWC), through the efforts of the Royal Police of Bhutan, and the NGO Respect, Educate, Nurture, and Empower Women (RENEW), the prevalence of night hunting incidents declined significantly. There were no reported incidents of the practice during the reporting period.

The law prohibits domestic violence. Penalties for perpetrators of domestic violence range from a prison sentence of one month to three years. Offenders are also fined the daily national minimum wage for 90 days. Police stated that they encouraged women to reconcile with their allegedly abusive husbands and couples to pursue mediation before they file criminal charges for domestic violence. Three police stations across the country housed women and child protection units to address crimes involving women and children and eight police stations housed desks with officers specifically devoted to women and children's issues. The government passed rules and regulations clarifying the Domestic Violence Act, trained police on gender issues, and allowed civil society groups to undertake further efforts, including operation of a crisis and rehabilitation center. The UN Committee on the Elimination of Discrimination against Women (CEDAW) expressed concern about reports of violence against women by their spouses or other family members and at work. According to the 2010 Bhutan Multiple Indicator Survey (BMIS), 68 percent of women believed certain behavior justified domestic violence. RENEW operated a domestic violence center in the capital. The Domestic Violence Prevention Act authorized the National Commission for Women and Children (NCWC) to develop and implement programs to prevent domestic violence, rehabilitate survivors, and conduct studies.

Sexual Harassment: The Labor Employment Act has specific provisions to address sexual harassment in the workplace. NGOs reported that these provisions were generally enforced.

Reproductive Rights: The country has no legal restrictions regarding the number, spacing, or timing of children, and there were no reports of coercion regarding reproduction. Modern contraception was available and legal. The UN Population Division estimated that 66 percent of women of reproductive age used a modern method of contraception in 2015. Women's rights NGOs noted that there were generally no prohibitions against women accessing sexual and reproductive healthcare. The World Bank reported that access and equity to medical care for pregnant women was a challenge because of difficult terrain, leading to disparities in access to skilled birth attendants linked to geography and wealth. According to the World Bank, World Health Organization, and other UN agencies, the maternal mortality ratio in 2015 was 148 and increased from 120 deaths per 100,000 live births in 2013. According to the UN Population Fund (UNFPA), 75 percent of births were attended by skilled health personnel.

Discrimination: The law provides for equal inheritance for sons and daughters. Traditional inheritance laws stipulate that inheritance is matrilineal and that daughters inherit family land and daughters do not assume their father's name at birth or their husband's name upon marriage. According to NGO and government sources, within the household, men and women enjoyed relatively equal status.

The law mandates the government take appropriate measures to eliminate all forms of discrimination and exploitation of women, including trafficking, abuse, violence, harassment, and intimidation, at work and at home, and the government generally enforced the law. CEDAW expressed concern that the constitution does not include prohibitions on both "direct and indirect" forms of discrimination. CEDAW also noted that the government failed to adopt implementing legislation for its international treaty obligations related to women's rights. The government said that provisions had been made in already existing legislation.

The NGO National Women's Association worked to improve women's living standards and socioeconomic status. RENEW, another NGO, also promoted and advocated for women's rights and political participation. The NCWC actively defended the rights of women and children during the year, working closely with the Ministry of Home and Cultural Affairs, the judiciary, and the police.

Children

<u>Birth Registration</u>: Under the constitution, only children whose parents are both citizens of Bhutan acquire Bhutanese citizenship at birth. The birth must be registered before the child turns one year old. According to the Bhutanese Refugee Support Group, existing citizenship laws caused certain children to be categorized as "non-nationals" (see section 2.d.). Births in remote areas were less likely to be registered. Children who do not acquire citizenship before turning one year old are able to petition the king for citizenship. The government provides health and education services for children without citizenship. However, children in this situation are not able to acquire nonobjection certifications, citizenship identification cards, and passports.

<u>Education</u>: The government provides 11 years of universal free education to children although education is not compulsory. While gender parity at the primary level has been achieved, distances to the country's secondary and tertiary schools, lack of adequate sanitation, and transportation difficulties contributed to girls' unequal access to secondary and higher education. The law requires proof of birth registration for children to attend school. Children of non-Bhutanese residents may enroll with a copy of a parent's work permit, employer letter, and documentation from the Department of Immigration.

<u>Child Abuse</u>: The law prohibits child abuse and provides for a minimum penalty of one year's imprisonment for perpetrators. Corporal punishment is banned in

schools, and there were no reported incidents in monasteries. Reports of child abuse were rare.

Early and Forced Marriage: The statutory minimum age of marriage for both men and women is 18. Statistics from the 2010 BMIS (the latest available) indicated that 31 percent of marriages occurred before age of 18 and 7 percent before age of 15. In 2010, 15 percent of girls and young women between the ages of 15 and 19 were either married or in a civil union. The National Health Survey of 2012 found that 24 percent of girls and young women between the ages of 10 and 24 were married or in a civil union, of which 3.7 percent were adolescents (age 10-19). The average age for a first pregnancy was reported between the ages of 20 and 22. While child marriage has become less common in urban areas, in remote villages there were reports of secret marriage ceremonies involving girls younger than 15. Child marriage took place in all regions, but the incidence was higher in the western and central areas of the country.

The government initiative Youth Friendly Health Services sought to prevent child marriage. It conducted community outreach and awareness campaigns to alert communities to the dangers of child marriage.

Sexual Exploitation of Children: The law prohibits sexual exploitation, including child pornography, child prostitution, the sale of children, and child trafficking. The legal age of consent is 16 for both boys and girls.

International Child Abductions: The country is not a party to the 1980 Hague Convention on the Civil Aspects of International Child Abduction. See the Department of State's *Annual Report on International Parental Child Abduction* at www.travel.state.gov/content/childabduction/en/legal/compliance.html.

Anti-Semitism

The country does not have a Jewish population, and there were no reports of anti-Semitic acts.

Trafficking in Persons

See the Department of State's *Trafficking in Persons Report* at www.state.gov/j/tip/rls/tiprpt/.

Persons with Disabilities

The constitution specifically protects the rights of citizens with disabilities. Legislation directs the government to attend to the security of all citizens in the "event of sickness and disability." The law stipulates that new buildings be constructed to allow access for persons with disabilities, but the government did not enforce this legislation consistently. There were reports that hospitals were generally accessible to persons with disabilities, but residential and office buildings were not.

Under the Disability Prevention and Rehabilitation Program, the government seeks to provide medical and vocational rehabilitation for persons with all types of disabilities, promote integration of children with disabilities in schools, and foster community awareness and social integration. There was no government agency specifically responsible for protecting the rights of persons with disabilities.

There were special-education institutes for students with disabilities, including the National Institute for the Disabled in Khaling, which educates children with vision disabilities, and an education resource unit in Paro for persons with hearing disabilities. Children with disabilities often attended mainstream schools although the resources needed to accommodate them varied among school districts. There also were special education facilities in Thimphu designed to meet the needs of children with physical and mental disabilities. Although there were no government-sponsored social welfare services available for persons with disabilities, the National Pension and Provident Fund granted benefits to such persons. Three NGOs, the Disabled Persons' Association of Bhutan, Ability Bhutan Society, and Drakstsho Vocational Center for Special Children and Youth, seek to change the public perception of disability and assisting persons with disabilities and their families.

According to the *Bhutan Observer*, in rural areas there was widespread discrimination against persons with disabilities, and some parents did not send children with disabilities to school.

National/Racial/Ethnic Minorities

Organizations in Nepal claimed that employers discriminated against Nepali-speaking Bhutanese seeking employment (see section 7.d.). The government claimed Nepali speakers were proportionally represented in civil service and government jobs.

English was the medium of instruction in all government schools. Dzongkha, the national language, was taught as an additional subject. Sharchopkha, Bumpthapkha, Khenkha, Nepali, and Tibetan were also spoken in the country. The UN Committee on the Rights of the Child expressed concern about the ability of minority children, specifically the Nepali-speaking minority, to maintain their cultural practices, observe their religion, or use their language.

Acts of Violence, Discrimination, and Other Abuses Based on Sexual Orientation and Gender Identity

The constitution guarantees equal protection of the laws and application of rights but does not explicitly protect individuals from discrimination for sexual orientation or gender identity. Laws against "sodomy or any other sexual conduct that is against the order of nature" exist. The penal code imposes penalties of up to one year in prison for engaging in prohibited sexual conduct. In response to recommendations to decriminalize same-sex sexual conduct during the country's Universal Periodic Review, the government stated the law "has never been evoked since its enactment for same-sex acts between two consenting adults. These provisions can be reviewed when there is a felt need for it by the general population."

The lesbian, gay, bisexual, transgender, and intersex (LGBTI) population has historically remained out of public view without an organized advocacy community. In 2014 several LGBTI groups established a public presence via social media. There were no NGOs in the country explicitly associated with LGBTI issues. There were no reports of violence directed against members of the LGBTI community although social bias occurred. In May, 13 LGBTI community members observed the International Day Against Homophobia, Biphobia and Transphobia (IDAHOT) and discussed their issues. An LGBTI community coordinator noted LGBTI Bhutanese continued to face stigmatization and discrimination. However, RENEW observed there had been a reduction in social stigma over the years.

A small transgender community existed, and transgender individuals faced social stigma although the community is gradually increasing its public visibility. The law does not provide any distinct legal status to transgender individuals, nor does it provide explicit protections.

HIV and AIDS Social Stigma

While NGOs claimed that there was no widespread HIV/AIDS-related stigma, observers noted that persons with HIV/AIDS did suffer from self-stigmatization and feared being open about their condition. One NGO, Lhak-Sam, was formed in 2010 and provides a network for persons with HIV/AIDS while working to reduce social stigma. Youth Development Fund, RENEW, and Chithuen Phendey Association work on this issue in collaboration with the Ministry of Health.

Persons with HIV/AIDS received free medical and counseling services, and the government maintained programs meant to prevent discrimination.

Section 7. Worker Rights

a. Freedom of Association and the Right to Collective Bargaining

The law provides for the right of workers to form and join independent unions. Workers can form a union with the participation of at least 12 employees from a single workplace. There is no national trade union. The law does not mention the right to conduct legal strikes. Most of the country's workforce engages in agriculture, a sector that is not unionized.

The law provides for the right of workers to bargain collectively with employers. The law prohibits antiunion discrimination and requires reinstatement of workers fired for union activity. Violators may face misdemeanor charges and be compelled to pay damages.

The government effectively enforced applicable laws. Resources, inspections, and remediation were adequate, and penalties for violations were sufficient to deter violations. The law grants workers the right to pursue litigation.

Freedom of association and the right to bargain collectively were respected although there were few employee unions. No unions were formed during the year.

The Ministry of Labor and Human Resources encouraged employee organization by conducting awareness-raising activities about employee rights during routine labor inspections. The government stated that associations of professional taxi drivers, truck drivers, and tour guides existed.

The Ministry of Labor and Human Resources, in its *Annual Report 2015-2016*, noted the areas of improvement on working conditions included an increase in the number of and conditions for labor inspectors.

The Ministry of Labor and Human Resources, in its *Annual Report 2015-2016*, noted that 24 labor inspectors conducted 2,434 inspections, issued 418 improvement and prohibition notices, and imposed 40 penalties. A total of 190 complaints were received, of which 185 resolved and five were pending at year's end. Nature of complaints received ranged from nonpayment of wages, termination without notice, resignation without notice, nonpayment of benefits, and other issues.

b. Prohibition of Forced or Compulsory Labor

The law prohibits most forms of forced or compulsory labor, and the government effectively enforced applicable laws. The law makes exceptions with regard to prison labor, work that might be required during an emergency, and work required for "important local and public" celebrations. The penal code criminalizes trafficking for illegal, but not exploitative, purposes. Violations of the labor law with respect to worst forms of child labor, forced and compulsory labor, improvement notice, prohibition notice, nonpayment of compensation, minimum age of admission into employment, employing foreigners without permit, and not complying with permits issued by the government are felonies subject to three to five years' imprisonment. Resources, inspections, and remediation were adequate, and penalties were sufficient to deter violations.

Government officials acknowledged there may be forced labor among domestic servants working in private homes where the Ministry of Labor and Human Resources has no jurisdiction. Officials relied on citizens to report forced labor of domestics directly to the police. Government officials acknowledged the rise of cross border human smuggling through illegal agents.

Migrant workers from India who worked in the country's construction and hydropower sectors and Indian women and girls who worked in domestic service or as caregivers were vulnerable to forced labor. Ministry of Labor and Human Resources noted there are approximately 54,000 migrant workers in the country, mostly from India. Young, rural citizens were transported to urban areas, generally by relatives, for domestic work, and some of these individuals were subjected to domestic servitude. There were unconfirmed reports that girls who worked as domestic servants and entertainers in "drayungs" (karaoke bars), were subjected to labor trafficking through debt and threats of physical abuse. The NAHRC conducted an investigation into "drayungs" and found no evidence of trafficking or forced labor.

Also see the Department of State's annual *Trafficking in Persons Report* at www.state.gov/j/tip/rls/tiprpt/.

c. Prohibition of Child Labor and Minimum Age for Employment

The minimum age for employment is 13 and the minimum age for hazardous work is 18. Children under the age of 18 are prohibited from working in dangerous occupations, including mining, construction, sanitary services, carpet weaving, or serving in bars. Under the Labor and Employment Act 2007, Section 9, on the prohibition of worst forms of child labor, violations are a felony offense with penalties ranging from with five to nine years' imprisonment.

Labor inspectors operating under the Ministry of Labor and Human Resources generally enforced child labor laws effectively. Resources, inspections, and remediation were adequate, and penalties were sufficient to deter violations. Under the Labor and Employment Act 2007, Section 9 on the prohibition of worst forms of child labor, a person guilty of that offense would be punished with five to nine years of non-bailable imprisonment.

Children performed agricultural and construction work, completed chores on family farms, or worked in shops and restaurants after school and during holidays. Child labor also occurred in hotels and automobile workshops. Girls were employed primarily as domestic workers, where they were vulnerable to abuse and exploitation. An estimated 19.6 percent of children between the ages of five and 14 were engaged in some form of child labor in 2011, which are the most current statistics. The BMIS established that 18.4 percent of the labor force in 2010 consisted of children under the age of 18. The 2013 Labor Force Survey undertaken by the Ministry of Labor and Employment counted 53,436 children between the ages of five and 17 employed in some form of labor.

Also see the Department of Labor's *Findings on the Worst Forms of Child Labor* at www.dol.gov/ilab/reports/child-labor/findings/.

d. Discrimination with Respect to Employment and Occupation

The law prohibits employment discrimination for employees and job applicants with respect to recruitment, dismissal, transfer, training, and demotion, but there were no distinctions of protected classes. The law also prescribes equal pay for equal work. In most cases, the government enforced these provisions. Employers who are convicted of discrimination are liable to pay a fine ranging from 360 to 1,080 times the daily national minimum wage (approximately $568 to $2,138). These penalties were generally sufficient to deter violations. Nepal-based organizations representing refugees claimed that Nepali-speaking Bhutanese were subject to discrimination with respect to employment and occupation (see section 6).

e. Acceptable Conditions of Work

The national minimum wage ranged from Nu 100 to Nu 125 ($1.58 to $1.98) per day. According to the government, all workers were above the minimum wage. The law defined the workday as eight hours per day with a one-hour lunch break, and employers were required to grant regular rest days. Work in excess of the legal workday must be paid at 1.5 times the normal rate. The official national poverty level was Nu 1,705 ($28) per month.

Occupational safety and health (OSH) standards are current and appropriate. Labor regulations grant workers the right to leave work situations that endanger their health and safety without jeopardy to their employment. All citizens are entitled to free medical care. At its expense the government transported persons who could not receive adequate care in the country to other countries (usually India) for treatment. Workers are eligible for compensation in the case of partial or total disability. Upon the death of a citizen, family members are entitled to compensation. The Ministry of Labor and Human Resources, in its *Annual Report 2015-2016*, noted monitoring of seven Health and Safety Committees was conducted and training on OSH imparted to 19 OSH Committees. An assessment of good OSH best practices was held for 55 committees of which 27 did not meet the standards.

The government generally enforced minimum wage, work hours, and occupational health and safety standards effectively in the formal sector. The law states that employers who fail to pay employees the correct amount of wages will be fined 90 times the national minimum wage for each violation (approximately $157). Employers who do not comply with work hours regulations will be fined 30 times the national minimum wage for the first violation (approximately $52), 90 times for the second violation (approximately $157), and 360 times for the third and each subsequent violation (approximately $630). Noncompliance with OSH standards is a felony and punishable by three to five years' imprisonment. These penalties were generally sufficient to deter violations. The lack of sufficient labor inspectors was a problem. The government employed 25 labor inspectors appointed to posts in Thimphu and four permanent regional offices that were assisted by technical experts. The government also posted labor inspectors to field offices located at major construction sites such as hydropower plant projects. According to a 2012 Ministry of Labor and Human Resources report compiled with the assistance of the World Health Organization, there were insufficient labor inspectors to cover the country's industries. In August five workers were buried in a landslide at the Mangdechu hydropower project when one side of the construction pit for the dam collapsed. The Ministry of Labor and Human Resources, in its *Annual Report 2015-2016*, noted a total of 60 accidents took place during the period, of which 24 were fatal, four led to complete disability, and 32 partial disability. Work place of accidents took place in the construction, hydropower, manufacturing and production, mining, and trading services sectors. Compensation was fully recovered in two cases, paid in three, under process in seven, partially done in one, partial payment in five, and there was no progress in three cases at year's end.